AMERICAN HEROES

# Jacob Lawrence

*A Painter's Story*

# JACOB LAWRENCE

## *A Painter's Story*

Clifton Park - Halfmoon Public Library
475 Moe Road
Clifton Park, New York 12065

SNEED B. COLLARD III

 **Marshall Cavendish**
Benchmark
New York

*To Barbara and Lisa*

Marshall Cavendish Benchmark
99 White Plains Road
Tarrytown, New York 10591
www.marshallcavendish.us

*Library of Congress Cataloging-in-Publication Data*
Collard, Sneed B.
Jacob Lawrence : a painter's story / by Sneed B. Collard III.
p. cm. — (American heroes)
Includes index.
Summary: "A juvenile biography of Jacob Lawrence, African-American painter"—Provided by the publisher.
ISBN 978-0-7614-4058-1
1. Lawrence, Jacob, 1917-2000—Juvenile literature.
2. African American painters—Biography—Juvenile literature.  I. Title.
ND237.L29C65 2009
759.13—dc22
[B]
2008034819

Editor: Joyce Stanton
Publisher: Michelle Bisson
Art Director: Anahid Hamparian
Series Designer: Anne Scatto
Printed in Malaysia
1 3 5 6 4 2

5035

©2008 The Jacob and Gwendolyn Lawrence Foundation, Seattle / Artists Rights Society (ARS), New York

Images provided by Debbie Needleman, Picture Researcher, Portsmouth, NH, from the following sources: *Front Cover:* Jacob Lawrence, c. 1950 *(detail)* Sid Bernstein, photographer/Riordan Studios. 1 photographic print: b&w; 26 x 21cm. Courtesy of the Jacob Lawrence and Gwendolyn Knight papers, 1945-1995 (bulk 1973-1994), Archives of American Art, Smithsonian Institution. *Back Cover:* Hirshhorn Museum and Sculpture Garden, Smithsonian Institution, Gift of Joseph H. Hirshhorn, 1966. Photograph by Lee Stalsworth. *Pages i, 34:* Jacob Lawrence, c. 1950 *(detail).* Sid Bernstein, photographer/Riordan Studios. Courtesy of the Jacob Lawrence and Gwendolyn Knight papers, Archives of American Art, Smithsonian Institution; *pages ii, vi, 15, 16, 19, 20, 32:* Photo: The Jacob and Gwendolyn Lawrence Foundation/Art Resource, NY; *page 3:* Photographs and Prints Division, Schomburg Center for Research in Black Culture, The New York Public Library, Aster, Lenox and Tilden Foundations; *page 4:* Jacob Lawrence, American (1917-2000). *Home Chores,* 1945. Gouache and graphite on paper, 29 ? x 29 1/16 in. (74.9 x 73.8 cm). The Nelson-Atkins Museum of Art, Kansas City, Missouri, Anonymous gift, F69-6. Photograph by Jamison Miller; *pages 7, 31:* ©Bettmann/CORBIS; *page 8:* Library of Congress Prints and Photographs Division Washington, D.C. (LC-USZ62-107551); *page 11:* ©Geneviere Naylor/CORBIS; *page 12:* Library of Congress Prints and Photographs Division, Washington D.C. (LC-USZC2-1110); *page 23:* The Phillips Collection, Washington, D.C.; *pages 24, 27:* Digital Image ©The Museum of Modern Art/Licensed by SCALA/Art Resource, NY; *page 28:* Jacob Lawrence (1917-2000). *Tombstones,* 1942. Gouache on paper, 28 ? x 20 ? in. (73.03 x 52.07cm). Whitney Museum of American Art, New York, Purchase 43.14

# CONTENTS

*Jacob's 1937 painting* Moving Day *reflects the uncertain—
and interesting—times that he lived through.*

*Jacob Lawrence*

Jacob Lawrence lived through some of our nation's hardest—and most interesting—times. He lived through a time when millions of people uprooted their lives and moved to new places. He lived through the Great Depression. He lived through the fear and excitement of World War II. But he rarely shared how he felt about these events. He did not have to. He let his paintings speak for him.

Jacob Lawrence was born during the Great Migration. From World War I until the start of World War II, more than one and a half million black Americans moved from southern states to the North. They came north to find jobs—and to escape prejudice. In the South, "Jim Crow" laws kept black people from voting, and from living as free and equal citizens. The Ku Klux Klan punished or killed black people who "stepped out of line." Good jobs were almost impossible to find.

*During the Great Migration, more than a million black Americans moved to the North.*

*Jacob's mother, Rosa Lee, worked hard to support her family.*

Like many others, Jacob's parents left the South to look for a better life. Lawrence's mother, Rosa Lee, came from Virginia. His father, Jacob, came from South Carolina. They met in Atlantic City, New Jersey. There, his mother did housework for other people. His father worked as a cook. Their son Jacob was born on September 7, 1917. He did not stay in Atlantic City for long. His parents took him to Easton, Pennsylvania. After several years there, his parents separated, and in 1924 his mother moved the family to Philadelphia.

By now, Jacob had a younger sister and brother, and their mother could not take care of the children by herself. She left them in foster care while she looked for work in New York City. Losing his parents and living with strangers must have been very hard for Jacob and his siblings. But in 1930 Rosa Lee brought her children to live with her in Harlem. Harlem was New York City's — and the nation's — most important black community. It was packed with people from all over America and the world. Art and culture flowered in this environment. Even after the Great Depression put millions of Americans out of work, Harlem swirled with new ideas. It was a perfect place for a young artist to grow up.

*In the 1930s, Harlem was one of America's most exciting cities—
especially for a budding artist.*

*Jacob began painting after school in one of Harlem's settlement houses.*

Jacob's interest in art began almost by accident. "My first exposure to art," he remembered, "was at an after-school settlement house." Settlement houses offered day care, meals, classes, and other services to poor people living in big cities. Since his mother worked all day, Jacob went to the settlement house after school. There, he began learning about arts and crafts.

The settlement house did not have fancy art supplies, but Jacob didn't care. Using crayons and poster paints, he made drawings and paintings with strong shapes and bright colors. "Our homes were . . . full of a lot of pattern, like inexpensive throw rugs," Jacob remembered. "Because we were so poor, the people used this as a means of brightening their life. I used to paint bright patterns after these throw rugs."

*Like these art students, Jacob painted the things and people around him.*

*The Works Progress Administration gave Jacob*
*a chance to learn from top artists and teachers.*
*This is a WPA advertisement.*

Others quickly saw that Jacob had a gift for art. During the Depression, President Franklin Roosevelt put many artists to work under the WPA—the Works Projects Administration. Jacob took art classes given by WPA art teachers. With money he earned doing odd jobs, he also rented space in an art studio called Studio 306. Studio 306 was an exciting place for a teenage boy. Some of the nation's best artists worked there. They gave him ideas and encouragement.

Jacob's painting style was influenced by other artists of his time, but he followed his own path. His art teacher, Charles Alston, said, "It would have been a mistake to try to teach Jake. He was teaching himself, finding his own way."

Jacob painted Harlem street scenes such as funerals. He painted rooms full of poor people living their daily lives. As before, he created bold designs and bright colors. Jacob did not switch to oil paints, like most other artists did. Instead, he kept using water-based paints and painted on small wooden boards. These methods made Jacob's work different and exciting.

*Jacob's bold, bright colors and lively scenes helped make his work stand out from others.*

*Jacob wanted to use his art to teach black people about their own history.*

In 1937, Jacob won a scholarship to study at the American Artists School in New York. The following year, the WPA hired him as a painter. Soon, he began taking his art in a new direction.

During the 1920s and 1930s, artists around the world focused on problems in society. Jacob did, too. He especially thought about how black people knew so little of their own history. "I've always been interested in history," Jacob explained, "but they never taught Negro history in the public schools." He decided to begin teaching black history with his art.

Jacob decided to paint about a man named Toussaint L'Ouverture. Toussaint had helped free the slaves on the island of Hispaniola. Like George Washington, he had led his people to create their own independent nation, the country of Haiti. Jacob read all about Toussaint at the public library. Then, he painted a series of forty-one pictures about Toussaint's life. Like his earlier works, each painting was bold and colorful. Jacob also described each painting in words. Together, the series told a complete story.

*Jacob's first series of paintings was about the life of Toussaint L'Ouverture, a former slave who freed the people of Haiti. In this picture, Jacob shows the cruelty the slaves endured on the plantations in Haiti.*

*One of Jacob's series captured the passion of anti-slavery activist Harriet Tubman.*
*As Jacob wrote, "She spoke in words that brought tears to the eyes and sorrow to the hearts*
*of all who heard her. . . ."*

Jacob decided to try his hand at other series. He painted thirty-two pictures about Frederick Douglass, a former slave who became a famous anti-slavery writer and speaker. Next, he painted a series about Harriet Tubman, another former slave who led other slaves to freedom. These series helped Americans see our history in new ways. But Jacob was only getting started.

For his next project, Jacob decided to paint a piece of his own history—the Great Migration. Jacob did not take part in the Great Migration himself, but his parents did. Over the years, he also watched thousands of other people arrive in Harlem from the South. "It was a great epic drama taking place in America," he later said. Jacob won scholarships to work on this important event. He read books about it. Then, he started painting.

*Jacob's most famous series of paintings showed the Great Migration —*
*to places like Chicago, New York, and St. Louis.*

*Brutal poverty and prejudice led to the Great Migration.*

*The Migration of the Negro* series included sixty different paintings. They showed the poverty and violence that black people faced in the South. They showed the people leaving their homes and traveling north. They showed the hope—and the hardships—people found in their new homes. In his series, Jacob did not paint each painting one at a time. Instead, he sketched and planned all of the paintings together. Then, he applied paint to all of the paintings at once, one color at a time. This helped the entire series seem more connected.

The Migration series was a major event in Jacob's career. An important art gallery in New York City started showing his work. A national magazine published twenty-four of the Migration paintings. Two large museums bought the Migration paintings for their collections. This was one of the first times a black artist had been given such attention. It was a breakthrough for black artists everywhere.

*Police tried to keep black people from leaving the South,*
*as Southerners became worried about a labor shortage.*

*Life in the North also had its hardships.*

In July 1941, Jacob married Gwendolyn Knight. Like Jacob, Gwen was an artist. She had helped him with his work, including the Migration series. After they married, Jacob completed a series about the famous anti-slavery figure John Brown. Then, he returned to painting about life in Harlem. The Harlem paintings are especially powerful. They show the struggles of individual people. Many have hunched-over bodies that show the hardships they are facing. Their eyes express sadness and fear, anger and determination.

Soon, though, Jacob would be swept up by world events.

At the end of 1941, the United States entered World War II. In October 1943, Jacob was drafted into the Coast Guard. Black soldiers faced a lot of prejudice in the military during World War II. They usually got the worst jobs. Jacob, though, got assigned to work as an artist, painting scenes of Coast Guard life. Other artists also painted the war, but Jacob's work is different. He did not paint battles and people dying. Instead, he painted the men at their everyday tasks. As always, he showed the human side of history instead of the big, flashy events.

*Jacob stands before one of his pictures at an exhibition of his work in Boston in 1945.*
*Jacob liked to paint ordinary people at their everyday tasks.*

*Jacob's paintings show the humanity we all share.*

By the time World War II ended, Jacob had become one of America's most important artists. He spent the next fifty years painting people and events he thought were important. He also taught other artists. He won many awards. His paintings were shown in museums around the world. But always, Jacob walked his own path. Until he died, on June 9, 2000, he stayed true to his own style—and his own desire to paint experiences that people everywhere have in common.

# IMPORTANT DATES

**1917** Born September 7 in Atlantic City, New Jersey.

**1924** Parents separate. Rosa Lee leaves children in foster care and moves to New York.

**1930** Rosa Lee brings Jacob, his brother and sister to Harlem; Jacob takes after-school art classes.

**1934** Studies art at WPA Harlem Art Workshop.

**1935** Begins painting everyday life in Harlem.

**1937** Gets scholarship to study at American Artists School.

**1938** Finishes first series of paintings, *The Life of Toussaint L'Ouverture*; hired by WPA to paint.

**1941** Completes series *The Migration of the Negro*; marries Gwendolyn Knight.

**1943** Drafted into U.S. Coast Guard during World War II.

**1970** Accepts position as full professor at the University of Washington in Seattle.

**1979** Appointed commissioner of the National Council of Arts by President Jimmy Carter.

**1983** Retires from teaching; elected to the American Academy of Arts and Letters.

**2000** Dies June 9 at the age of 82, at home in Seattle.

# WORDS TO KNOW

**Depression** Also called the Great Depression; a time in America during the 1930s when many businesses failed and many people lost their jobs.

**drafted** To be called into service, usually by the military.

**epic drama** A long story or poem celebrating the great deeds and adventures of a people.

**foster care** Care of children in a home that is not a relative's.

**Great Migration** The movement of millions of black Americans from the South to other parts of the country. They went to find jobs and escape prejudice.

**Jim Crow laws** Laws created especially to keep black people from voting and from having equal rights with other citizens.

**Ku Klux Klan** A secret organization of white people who used threats and violence to prevent African Americans from gaining equal rights.

**Negro** A name that was used in the past for people of African descent; a black person.

**plantation** A large estate or farm worked by laborers who live there.

**prejudice** Treating or viewing people unfairly simply because of their skin color or their religion or something else that makes them seem different.

**scholarship** Money that is given to a student to help pay for his or her studies.

**Works Projects Administration** One of several government agencies that created work for people during the Great Depression.

# To Learn More about Jacob Lawrence

## WEB SITES

*The Jacob and Gwen Lawrence Virtual Resource Center*
**http://www.jacobandgwenlawrence.org/**
*Jacob Lawrence: Exploring Stories*
**http://www.whitney.org/jacoblawrence/**
*Schomburg Center for Research in Black Culture,* "In Motion"
**http://www.inmotionaame.org/migrations/index.cfm**

## BOOKS

*The Great Migration: An American Story* by Jacob Lawrence.
HarperCollins Children's Books, 1995.

*Harriet and the Promised Land* by Jacob Lawrence. Simon &
Schuster Children's Publishing, 1997.

*Story Painter: The Life of Jacob Lawrence* by John Duggleby and
Jacob Lawrence. Chronicle Books, 1998.

*Toussaint L'ouverture: The Fight for Haiti's Freedom* by Walter Dean
Myers. Simon & Schuster Children's Publishing, 1996.

## PLACES TO VISIT

The Phillips Collection (Museum)
1600 21st Street, NW
Washington, DC 20009
PHONE: (202) 387-2151
WEB SITE: http://www.phillipscollection.org/

Seattle Art Museum Downtown
1300 First Avenue
Seattle, WA 98101-2003
PHONE: (206) 654-3100
WEB SITE: http://www.seattleartmuseum.org/

Whitney Museum of American Art
945 Madison Avenue at 75th Street
New York, NY 10021
PHONE: (800) 944-8639 WEB SITE: http://www.whitney.org

To find other locations of Jacob Lawrence art, see the
*Artcyclopedia* Web site: http://www.artcyclopedia.com/artists/
lawrence_jacob.html

# INDEX

# A Note on Quotes

THE QUOTES IN THIS BOOK come from two sources. One is an interview conducted with the artist by Carroll Greene on October 26, 1968. The second source is the book *Jacob Lawrence: American Painter* by Ellen Harkins Wheat (University of Washington Press, 1986), which contains additional interview excerpts. In most cases, I did not include entire quotations, but only those words that were important to what I was writing about.

—SNEED B. COLLARD III

# ABOUT THE AUTHOR

**SNEED B. COLLARD III** is the author of more than fifty award-winning books for young people, including *Science Warriors*; *Wings*; *Pocket Babies*; and the four-book *SCIENCE ADVENTURES* series for Marshall Cavendish Benchmark. In addition to his writing, Sneed is a popular speaker and presents widely to students, teachers, and the general public. In 2006, he was selected as the Washington Post–Children's Book Guild Nonfiction Award winner for his achievements in children's writing. He is also the author of several novels for young adults, including *Dog Sense, Flash Point,* and *Double Eagle.* To learn more about Sneed, visit his Web site at www.sneedbcollardiii.com.